Spirits Do Not Fear Death

Spirits Do Not Fear Death
A Poetry Collection

Chinomso Onyinye Ezeh

Published by Spines
Isbn: 979-8-89569-296-7

Contents

Spirits Do Not Fear Death

Chinomso Onyinye Ezeh

chi/chi/

noun

In the religious concept of the Igbo[1] people of Nigeria:

1. A personal spirit being or god assigned to each person by the supreme God, *Chi Ukwu*
2. A spirit guardian believed to be responsible for a person's fortunes and misfortunes in life

"The Igbo believe that a man receives his gifts or talents, his character – indeed his portion in life generally – before he comes into the world. It seems there is an element of choice available to him at that point; and that his *chi* presides over bargaining."

Achebe, Chinua. 'Chi in Igbo Cosmology.' *Morning Yet on Creation Day*. London: Heinemann, 1975, pp. 131-145

1. A person's spirit-double; a person's other identity in the spirit world

"In a general way, we may visualize a person's *chi* as his other identity in spiritland – his *spirit being* complementing his terrestrial *human being*; for nothing can stand alone, there must always be another thing standing beside it."

Achebe, Chinua. 'Chi in Igbo Cosmology.' *Morning Yet on Creation Day*. London: Heinemann, 1975, pp. 131-145

[1]The Igbo people inhabit southeastern Nigeria. Igbo refers to both the people and their language.

For my *chi*

Chi m nọ m nso
'My *chi* is with me'
Always
Let me tell you about my *chi*
My personal god
The protector of my past
The curator of my present
The determiner of my future
My faithful cheerleader
My honest critic
Fiery and fierce
Kind and loving
Fluid through the ebbs and flows
Her abundant love is amplified to degrees that
Rock my world in ways that scare most mortals
My anchor in turbulent times
She keeps me grounded
Fortified under the glory of her divine favor
My *chi* is with me
Now and always.

Onye kwe, chi ya ekwe.

'Whatever one agrees to, their *chi* will move in accordance to.'

Igbo Proverb

Part One

Mmiri Na-eri

The Drowning

Repossessing Our Identity (I)

Yesterday, I wanted to ask
Will we cower in fear
Let the darkness consume us
When our *chi* is all shades of light
Stand still until the hatred attacks
A storm of injustice rages on the horizon
Mindlessly, wallowing in ignorance
Of the might of our *chi*
Robbed of our humanity
Our right to live in truth
As one with our *chi*

When will we take back our strength
Our rightful place among the stars
When will we take back our voice
Let our *chi* speak life with
A strong, sonorous, piercing voice
To say no more
Will we ever fully inhabit our bodies
No shame or fear
But with pride and belief
In the sustenance of our *chi*
Will we ever fight back
With actual fists
Leave a trail of impact

I wanted to ask
Will this drowning be our end
But that was yesterday.

Good Women

Good women make sacrifices
She wanted to be good
So she gave herself
Over and over again

She gave her freedom
Gave her ambition
Gave her sanity
Until there was nothing left to give
Nothing except her voice
But her *chi* would not be silenced
So they plotted and robbed her from within.

Old Soul

Her young back is ridden with scars
That tell tales of an old broken soul

Her young back is barely covered
By tatters of wrecked clothes
That speak to the magnitude of her suffering

Her young back is bent over in despondency
That proves the futility of her struggle

You wonder how a young one
Could experience more years than she has lived
How her vibrant youthfulness
Could turn into this display of grotesque

The answer lies
In the weft of her patched skin attempting to heal
Her *chi* is weaving
In the recoiling of her frame
Heeding to the sensibility of her *chi*
In the coldness of her hesitant touch
Her *chi* will not lose guard
In the deep-rooted distrust lurking in her eyes
Her *chi* is no stranger to mistrust
In the fixed gaze of her sunken sockets
Allowing her *chi* to keep watch
In the surrender echoing in her absent voice
Her *chi* will speak for her
In the angry furrow of her brows

Rage consumes her *chi*
In the contortion of her face in sheer disgust
For those who underrate the extent of her *chi's* resolve

Her young mind is ridden with unforgivable cruelties
That tell tales of an old broken soul.

Enigma

She was lost to herself
Drowned by the uncertainty surrounding her essence
Subdued by obscure fragments of her identity
She hid behind the enigma of her *chi*
Refused to delve into a deeper understanding
Of her *chi's* narrative
Behind her sense of self

She shielded herself with a web of mystery
Into which her entire being
Appeared to be meticulously woven
A maze, unfamiliar to her
Yet known to her *chi*

Protect the heart
From those who would hastily covet it
With no understanding of its operations
From herself
Who might expose it to heartache
These words never left her consciousness
They persisted in her *chi's* keen mind

But how was her *chi* to protect a heart
That lay submerged in a sea of fear
A fear, all too familiar to the ageless divinity
Distrust whispered words of damnation into her ears
Disappointment beckoned to her at every turn

So she stayed in her prison
Locked in by the mystery of who she was
Who her *chi* is
Her eyes reflect an intense warning
To all who care to take heed
Do not try to look past the enigma of her *chi*
That powerful presence you sense
She can't save you from herself.

Misconstrued

Worldly assumptions cling to you
Like they define your place in the world
Your feelings, dreams, sense of purpose
The very essence of who you are
Destabilized by the judgment of people
Who know only what this flawed society permits

Scoundrels test your consciousness
In the bodies of seemingly well-meaning folks
And your strength of character
Left at the mercy of wolves in sheep's clothing
Silently, fatally devouring your self-esteem

Now you're lost
Lost to the people around you
Lost to yourself
A shadow of what you could have been
With your *chi*
Should have been
With your *chi*
Oblivion
Consciousness
Panic
Disappointment
If only they knew
If only you knew
What your *chi* knows
Then perhaps, you could begin to see yourself again

Find yourself again
Hope, a flicker in the distant clouds
Of an unending night
Focus, maybe you can wish it closer.

15

Out of Control

You loathe it
The heaviness that lies at the bottom of your belly
Proving futile your *chi's* attempts to expel it
You dread it
The weight that keeps you glued to your bed
Unable
No, unwilling to move a muscle
Even when your *chi* wills you to rise
You fear it
The darkness that could consume you one day
Cut you off from your *chi*

But more than anything else
You hate it
The helplessness
That accompanies each dreary episode

So you scheme and plan and plot
To take charge
To take back
Your agency
Even if the journey ends
With your end.

The Danger of Untested Feelings

Lost in the quest
For fulfillment
Of an earnest desire
She failed to check her soul
Against lurking dangers
Of which her *chi* foretold
In this predatory world
Forgot to keep her heart hidden
From the claws of untested feelings

That would leave her stranded
She underestimated the need to
Submit to her *chi's* restraint and
Balance her raging emotions
She let them run wild
Until it was too late to tame them
She let herself get swept away by
Wild currents of toxic affection
That left her eroded from
The tireless friction

Now she's wading through the murk
Barely breathing enough to
Stay grounded.

No Such Thing as Perfection

Even with this strength from my *chi*
There's a hint of weakness
How much longer can I
Hold on to these virtual truths

Even with this determination to rise with my *chi*
There's a chance of drowning
How much longer can I
Float in this sea of dissatisfaction

My *chi's* optimistic approach to life is
Still haunted by pessimistic probabilities
How much longer can I confess
These fictitious narratives of hope
My *chi's* progress is
Threatened by possible losses
How much longer can I
Avoid the depressing path of failure

This faith in my *chi's* vision of love
Remains tainted by doubt
How much longer can I
Believe in a love that truly sets free

When will I be free
To feel unloved but still allow love
To fail and still believe in success
To feel hopeless but still embrace hope
To fall and still rise
To be weak but still try to be strong
When will I set myself free
To be perfectly imperfect?

Hide to Live Another Day

Today, the dark cloud returned
And I lost touch with my *chi*
Only for a brief moment
But it was ominous enough to
Drag me into its lifeless bosom
I sank into the void
Without protest
Eyes fixated on my chi's fading frame

I cried until my eyes tired out
But the cloud wouldn't budge
These futile tears are exhausting
Incapable of eliminating the darkness
Today, the darkness showed its face
Again, I hid mine with
The haste of a frightened prey
Separated from my *chi*, my protector

My heart is still too heavy
I hide to live another day.

What Comes After

I've been on the run for too long
Trapped in an endless marathon
Always a grasp away from my *chi's* potential
Trying to escape this chilling grasp
Trapped in a disordered mind
In the embrace of chaos

Some days, an escape seems viable
Look well enough, there's a light from my *chi*
But that hope soon dims
Fear grabs me by the neck
I choke on the emptiness
I have no more to lose

Stuck existing
Forced to entertain empty connections
Leading to empty promises
Meaning is lost without my *chi*
Silhouettes where real people should be
Fiction where reality should be

Running, I'm still running
To whatever comes after.

Sometimes, I Fall

Sometimes, the world spins too fast
I lose my balance
Fall flat on my back
My eyes spasm in
Dubious attempts to
Make out the blur of
My *chi*
My ears throb
Frantic from
Gushes of whirlwind
My *chi* breezes past
Racing images of
Obscure figures
Hasty sounds of
Indistinct voices
A cacophony of chaos
Hostile to my *chi*
Dizzy, I succumb to
The thrust of gravity
And I fall flat on my back
How you found me.

Locked In

These walls around me have stood
For as long as
I've been conscious of
What it means to feel
They sprung from a subconscious
Of my *chi's* defensive nature
Tired of nursing a distressed soul
From the battering of incessant letdowns

Sometimes my *chi* takes a peek
Through the breaches
I let my mind run scared with
Thoughts of lurking dangers
Beyond the walls
Other times, I wonder
If I'm missing out on
The chilling thrill of
Living on the edge of heartbreak
Still, I can't bring myself to
Venture beyond these walls.

Caught Off-Guard

There are still unfortunate moments
When I find my consciousness hijacked
My *chi*'s firmness permeated
By imposing thoughts of the goodness
That I so desperately sought out
Beneath the glaring cruelty
Of this world

In these moments
I hold my breath
Hope my *chi* will
Whisk the memories away
But like the rapid gasps that ensue
When I can no longer remain breathless
The memory of the charade
Smothering my perspective
Inevitably pierces through my defenses.

Turbulent Identities

I was a yarn
Of turbulent identities
Hastily woven
By a desperate need
To appear whole

Can my *chi* maneuver multiplicity?

I was a conflux
Of baffling desires
Constantly unsettled
By the flow
Of puzzling passions

Will my *chi* wade through the complexity?

I was a cocktail
Of poisonous conventions
Skillfully mixed
By a tortuous desire
For unity

Can my *chi* unite these conflicting beliefs?

I was a volatile compound
Unstable yet at peace
With my turbulent soul.

What Used to Be

When you look into my eyes
Do you see the dying embers
Of what used to be
My fiery *chi*
Floating in a vacant chamber
That once was home
To a firmament of intensities
Which kept me grounded
Rooted in the promise of fulfillment

When you look into my eyes
Do you see the tainted memories
Of what used to be
My timeless *chi*
Buried underneath bogus new memories
That now house a tame personality
Lacking the vigor that marks my *chi*
Who kept me grounded
Rooted in the promise of fulfillment.

Unforgivable

Suffocating in a void
Threatened by a heavy emptiness
Pervading my body
Melancholic chills ring
Through the air
I can't feel my *chi's* sublime presence
Thrust into an abyss of infernal suffering
Abandoned to a fate of despair
As I struggle to breathe
Where is my comforter?

My sorrows plotted to
Snuff the life out of me
My *chi* beckons with warmth
But I search for redemption
In the deceitful remarks that
Hopeful strangers threw at me
I find only rotten speech
Breeding misery and destruction
Mocking my weakness
Where is my protector?

I would give up
Sink into the prickly arms of expiry
But my *chi* will not forgive me
For giving up her faith in me.

Who Decides Fate?

Who decides when the waves
Of emptiness hit us
When we find our minds
Plagued with harrowing suspicions
And demented spirits
Whisper reinforcements of self-pity
Overshadowing our *chi's* assurances

Who decides when the wind
Of gloom hits us
When we find our ears overwhelmed
By convincing arguments of our unworthiness
And uncouth mouths
Scream crudities of self-loathing
Drowning out our *chi's* affirmations

How do we stop ourselves
From being dragged
With malicious intent
Into the bottomless pit
From whence these foul-spirited mouths were forged?

Disappointment

Disappointment is like rain
Sometimes it descends gently
Fostering our guts
Awakening our *chi*
Watering seeds of hope
That lay dormant for years

Disappointment is like rain
But sometimes it floods our lives
Drowning our dreams
Quenching our *chi's* fire
Dismantling the anchors
That prevented our drifting

Disappointment is like rain
Who's to decide
If it spatters us gently
Spurring our growth
Or if it smacks us violently
Draining the spirit of our *chi* from us?

Part Two

Nke ịlụ ọgụ

The Struggle

Repossessing Our Identity (II)

Today, I realized I might be too late
The darkness is already upon us
And it has stripped us
Of our sense of direction
When our *chi* calls us by name,
The shady clouds do not waver

Now we're lost to our *chi*
Wanderers in the darkness
Crashing into each other
Hurting our bond with our *chi*
Hitting, hating
Like untamed animals

We're constantly attacked
By contempt of our truth
And it has turned us
Into self-loathing misfits
Flinching from our reflection
A poor replica of our *chi's* vision
We want to be everything
Everyone except ourselves

Believing false narratives
Shame has infiltrated our borders
Corrupting our sense of self-worth
Tainting our identities
We have been robbed of our humanity
Our right to live
In our truth
As one with our *chi*.

A Woman's Place

They stuff us into a box of lazy stereotypes
They say, "This is your place!
Stay in your place!"
I want to ask, "Why is it my place?
Has my *chi* chosen this place?"

They speak with false authority
Ignorant, simple-minded
Championing our stagnation
The delusion of their superiority
Will be their doom

Has my *chi* not warned them
That a woman's place is wherever she wants to be
That I will only fill spaces that soothe me
I will modify boxes to contain my *chi*
My place is wherever my *chi* chooses to be.

Conspiracy

Women are fragile creatures
They'll break in the face of pressure
Women are too emotional
They lead with their hearts, not their heads
So keep them under control
Never let them take the reins

But my *chi* is more than delicate.

A woman's place is in the home
She must keep her husband
Bear children, cater to her family
Live for everyone else but herself
Keep her subservient
As a supporter, never as a leader

But my *chi* is more than subordinate.

It's the greatest conspiracy
Prejudiced systems woven over time
Power and control
Fear of the unknown
What havoc will my *chi* cause when she is set free?
Or do they know?
Do they know how high I will fly with my *chi* when I am
free?

A Heart That Feels

Vulnerable to emotions
They spit out these words
Like a curse
But my *chi* has taught me
That vulnerability stems from
Depths of immense courage
To bare oneself to
Shades of uncertainty
Familiar and unfamiliar
And emerge victoriously
Not hiding from one's humanity
But embracing mortality
A heart that feels is no less important
Than a head that thinks.

The Other Side of Self-Confidence

Never quite right
Never enough
Never needed
Never wanted
Words never spoken
But implied at every turn
Tearing away at your flesh
One experience at a time

Don't you tire of the inadequacy
Your doubting mind
Keeps you trapped in
Have you wondered
What it feels like
To exist on
The other side of self-confidence
How long will you watch yourself
Fade from continuous letdowns
Existing as a shadow of
The potential your bones carry

Where is your *chi?*
Don't you feel her
Gnawing at your skin
Desperate to escape this
Sham of weakness you hide behind
A mist of effeminate power
Seeping from your pores

If you stay submerged in subservience
Your *chi* will drag you
All the way if she must
To the other side of self-confidence.

39

A Vicious Cycle

Our eyes have run out of tears
Tears for our stifled dreams
Our mouths are weary from wailing
Mourning our shunned ambition
Our noses writhe at the stench of loss
Loss of our will to fight
Our hearts ache from the weight of perceived failure

We retreat into the solitude of our pain
Where our *chi*'s healing hands swing into action
She speaks life into us
Somewhere amid this hurt
Hope lies in wait
Our *chi*, a resilient star in the distant sky
A hidden gem in the earth beneath our feet
So we glue our faces to the sky
With bare hands, we dig the earth
But all we see are lightning bolts in the sky
Threatening to strike what remains of us
And quicksand into which our shallow frames sink
Panic
Running
Hiding
Screaming
Falling
Hope
Repeat
It's a vicious cycle.

Dissatisfied

She viewed the world with a dissatisfaction that
Left her porous
Her life was never enough
No, it was never fully hers
And she didn't fight to possess it
What is for her *chi* is also for her

Navigating the world stuck with a life
She felt no connection to
But she could fall back
On her mind's intense ability
To provide a more suitable reality
Catering to her parched spirit

Retreat into the trusted arms
Of her spirit double
Going through the motions of a life
Others truly believed was hers alone
Her body present in the world
Through the years
Her soul, ravishing
The intimacy of her preferred reality
Her spirit identity flourishing
Where her humanity hesitated

It was her secret
One with which she was content to revel alone
The solitude was bliss
Until it wasn't.

Haunted

Genuine worry has begun to surface
Slowly emerging from
Divergent emotions
You've played with all these years
Like rain, resting in clouds
Teases an orphaned tadpole
Stranded in a shrinking pond
Worry watched you all these years
While your *chi* hibernates
Teasing with sparse bouts of relief
Waiting for the perfect moment
To strike at your *chi*
To show you who's really in control
Threatening thoughts you stifled all these years
Have sprung with a vengeance
Gnawing away at your self-esteem
Your confidence is torn apart
By claws of self-doubt
Recurring nightmares haunt your sleep
Repeated echoes of the uncertainty
Ring in your ears
Your *chi* is in distress
But her voice remains loud and crisp
"Do you think you can ever escape this haunting
If you do not face it?"

Beyond the Darkness

You have inhabited this darkness
For too long
Light has become a bane to your existence
So when your *chi* says
The sun will rise again
You flinch in fear

Your soul has wandered
For too long
Rest has become an uneasy burden
So when your *chi*
Wills you peace
You silently denounce it

Your body has borne
So much shame
Honor has become unsuited to you
So when your *chi* guides you
Into respected places
You lash out in bitterness

Your bones have grown
Accustomed to the hurt
Relief is now a discomfort
So when your *chi* promises
To shield you from pain
You plot ways to self-sabotage

You've been put down
So many times
Upliftment seems a lifetime away
So when your *chi*
Rewards your efforts
You deny the glory

The darkness is all you know
But you do not know everything
So when your *chi* promises better days
You may not know it
You may not believe it
Your *chi* knows
She believes for you
Hope abounds beyond the darkness.

Divine Intervention

She was uninterested
In the preacher's hysterical presentations
Ramblings of a mind too close-minded to
Appeal to the duality of a
Wandering soul like her

She was unperturbed
By his many theatrical doomsday proclamations
The hell he spoke of
Haunted her *chi's* existence
Till she fled from her steadfast spirit

So, like all other days
She sat before the preacher,
Her mind enchanted in a distant daze
Her sensibilities far-flung from the religious teacher
Fixated on reconnection with her *chi*

Until the word jolted her back to reality
Loneliness, the sneaky imp!
A prayer against this dubious spirit
That whispered seductive falsehoods
Drowning out her *chi's* affirmations
And tagging her unlovable

At that moment,
Belief was stirred up inside of her.
Faith was planted in the fertile soil of her heart

She gazed at the preacher
And for the first time
She saw the power beyond his physicality
She saw supreme divinity
Her *chi*, basking in infinite glory.

A Possibility of Hope

Running yourself headfirst
Into a fatal wreckage
You thought you were ready to
Embrace your *chi* beyond this life
But as you take in those final breaths
You hesitate
And think of living
On this side of existence
Your *chi* responds in flashes of hope

You cannot undo the wreck you've become
But you want to live
For your *chi*
In that moment, it's all that matters
Clinging to life
They say, "When there's life, there's hope"
You don't believe it
But someday, you might
This is what matters
This possibility of believing in hope
Grace
Goodness
Love
All of which your *chi* exudes
This possibility surpasses the bleakness
Consuming your mind
And it will save you.

Part Three

Nnupụisi Ahụ

The Awakening

Repossessing Our Identity (III)

Today, I realize the struggle may never end
The darkness will not shrink
Or make way for our *chi* to shine forth
In this bleak world
We will need to learn
To embrace our *chi's* devotion
To lean on our *chi's* resilience
To follow our *chi's* path
One step at a time
Patience sitting pretty on our shoulders
As we progress together
Never alone

Succeeding despite the odds
Self-deprecation will linger
So we must suit up in our *chi's* armor
Of self-respect and self-love
Drown any hostility
With devotion to our *chi's* divine influence
That keeps us bonded
The shame might never retreat
But the goodness in us will serve as our guide
We must take back what is ours
Our right to live our truth
It's not too late
To take back ownership of ourselves
Our *chi* is waiting.

Phantom Love

The shadows cannot contain me anymore
I no longer exist in the abstract recess of your mind
Now, I occupy space in your actuality
Chi m nọ m nso
My *chi* is with me
As I take my first breath of relief
The validity of my existence hits me
Greatness burns underneath my skin
I cannot go back to living in the shadows
So I look forward to your guidance
But you have become distant
Almost as if you wish I was still an abstraction
Perhaps, you loved the idea of what I could be
And not the reality of who I am.

The Last Straw

The last straw that broke the camel's back
Was not as visible as you'd expect
Nor was it the shameless display of disregard you anticipated
Waiting with high hopes
That she'd finally wake from the delusion

The last straw that broke the camel's back
Was more subtle than a lion stalking its prey
More hidden than a splinter of wood
Waiting to pierce the succulent skin of its next victim
More at home than a shark in the ocean

The last straw that broke the camel's back
Was a silent awakening within her fiery loins
The powerful presence of her *chi*
An internal uproar from the pit of her belly
The thundering echo of her *chi*
A decisive reminder of her name
The confidence of her *chi*
A determination with all the strength in her bones
To abandon mediocrity
To step into her queendom.

A Woman's Choice

Woman
Existing only in relation to others
Incapable of existing
Independently of her use to others
Helpmate
Wife
Mother
Labels that should support her
But end up limiting her
Inciting her *chi* to a place of rage
Contempt lurking in her gut
If only they understood
That helping isn't gender-specific
That marriage is an option
Not a necessity
Motherhood should be a choice
A woman's choice.

I'm Not Afraid to Feel

I'm not afraid to feel
The excitement
I'll sway to the upbeat
The numbness
I won't resist the anguish
I'll let this body vibrate to rhythms
Of organized chaos upon which life hinges
Let my *chi* relish the dissonance
There isn't always peace in order
Happiness doesn't always follow victory

I'm not afraid to feel
The satisfaction
I'll sway to the euphoria
The disappointment
I won't avoid the misery
I'll let my body embrace strokes
Of life's temperamental flare
Let my *chi* indulge the instability
The highs haul me to heights of pleasure
Rocking my entire world
And the lows keep me grounded
In the fragility of my existence.

What It Means to Live

Let me tell you what it feels like to
Come face-to-face with your *chi*
To finally break free from
That cage of incompatible existence
That trap of false principles
That confinement of mental stagnation
Those shackles of limited expression

It is like a new beginning
A second chance to know your *chi*
Like being born anew
This time, on your terms
The abundance of your *chi*
Ushering you into a new reality

It is like seeing the sunrise for the first time
Feeling its first rays kiss your skin to rejuvenation
Feeling the life permeate your bones
Your *chi* is a giver of life
Abundant life
Coming face to face with happiness
Falling in love with yourself anew
It is like finally living.

Spirits Do Not Fear Death

How does it feel to know you bear no part
In the blossoming of this flower?
While you plot to
Keep her in the dark
Her *chi* seeks other ways to
Illuminate her path

You present yourself
As an illusion of necessary sustenance
But her *chi* maintains her life force
You force her to cling to
Your toxic self
Breathing an overdose of
Your poisonous air
Surviving on the bile
You feed her

And her *chi* purges her
Cleanses her of your filth
Feeds her with optimistic promise
You plant seeds of falsehood in her mind
Conditioning her to believe that
Without you is death
You kept her dead
Or so you thought
But how can spirits fear death?
One with her *chi*
Her *chi* is not afraid of death.

Wisdom Chose Me

For the first time, I saw wisdom
In its true form
Memories of precious truths
Beyond my comprehension
Truths my *chi* whispers into my ears
Indescribable omens of things to come
Promises my *chi* lights my path with

A glance into the future
Spurred by experiences of the past
Wounds of an ugly past
My *chi* nurses with great diligence
An understanding of the communion
Between past, present, and future
Accumulated knowledge of
The workings of the universe
Insight into the whispers of elemental forces
Shaping our world
In ways I can hardly fathom

I saw wisdom
In the compelling eyes of my *chi*
Baring parts of myself
I'm too scared to explore
Urging me to listen more intensely
To the sacred spirits
Sworn to protect my essence
And pay homage in respect and awe of all

That exists beyond my limited sight
Wisdom chooses to whom it reveals itself
My *chi* said yes
And wisdom chose me.

The Relevance of Seasons

My *chi* is like a lonesome moon in the distant sky
Steadily dotting over this weary child
Through the excesses of the sun's rays
My *chi* shelters me
And the playful glee of the stars
My *chi* holds my hands
Enduring the gloom of countless storms
My *chi* is graceful, watchful
Magnificent in her simplicity

Towering above in the distant sky
Yet intimate to my feelings
My *chi* reveals to my curious mind
The relevance of seasons
Through which her guidance never wavers
Seasons of accentuated darkness
Of minimal light
Of partial beam
Of complete illumination

My *chi* is like a lonesome moon in the distant sky
She is proof that darkness comes and
An assurance that light will always shine through the
darkness.

Fulfillment Over Appeal

My *chi* affirms
In time, I will embrace the parts of myself
That push against mindless conformity
And stimulate questions of enlightenment
That the elders once hushed
In time, I will appreciate the shades of my character
That I was not taught to love
Unrefined parts of myself
I was forced to conceal
For fear of societal mockery
Uneven edges to my personality
That I cannot fit into any defined box
My identity as mortal and spirit

My *chi* affirms
The appeal of mainstream performance
These shimmers that tickle my fancy
Will eventually give way to the fulfillment of reality
The peace of living and breathing my truth.

I Am Worthy

Before I thought he was worthy
I was already worthy
Before I thought she was needed
I was already needed
Before I thought they were loved
I was already loved
My purpose is as certain as my *chi's* tenacity

Because my *chi* is joyous
I am worthy of happiness
Because my *chi* is steadfast
I am needed for good reason
Because my *chi* is gracious
I am loved

So why do I save my best affection for others
While I grovel for the remnants of my damn love
Before I knew it, my *chi* knew me
She knew that I was worthy
I still am
I am worthy of my damn love!

We Move

Five monumental steps forward with my *chi*
Took us long enough but
We're moving!
We feel the energy surge through our joints
Ready to go the full length of this race
But first, let me breathe
Breathe in, breathe out
One more time
Let's go!

A million quick steps backward
So sudden, I didn't even feel the movement
We've regressed!
I can feel my joints
Weaken with discouragement
I'm not ready to run
The same race twice
But quitting is not in my *chi's* nature

First, let us hold the culprits accountable
Those who smear dirt on our efforts
Who abhor our progress
Never give them peace
Chi, let's go!

Promises From My *Chi*

This gaping hole no other personality can fill
Will be filled with an unquestionable richness of character
These painful gaps in my memory
Strengthening their hold as I attempt to move on
Will resurface as joyful memories
This missing beat in the rhythm of my heart
Will become a soulful melody

My *chi* has spoken
So shall it be

My *chi* speaks life into my journey
The frailty living in my bones
Will be displaced by inexplicable strength
The throbbing threatening my joints
Will give way to ripples of comfort
The words pressed upon my thirsty lips
Will give way to generous blessings
The embrace eluding my cold skin
Will become my lasting warmth
The passion my spirit craves
Will be the reality I wake up to
And the sweet dreams that rock me to sleep
The love my doubtful mind hopes for
Will find me and never leave me
I will be whole again

My *chi* has spoken
And so shall it be.